Grade
4

Reading Comprehension

en by **Shannon Keeley**

Illustrations by **Jackie Snider**

FlashKids
An imprint of Sterling Children's Books

This book belongs to

_____

FLASH KIDS, STERLING, and the distinctive Sterling logo are registered trademarks of
Sterling Publishing Co., Inc.

Published by Sterling Publishing Co., Inc.
387 Park Avenue South, New York, NY 10016
Text and illustrations © 2007 by Flash Kids
Distributed in Canada by Sterling Publishing
c/o Canadian Manda Group, 165 Dufferin Street
Toronto, Ontario, Canada M6K 3H6
Distributed in the United Kingdom by GMC Distribution Services
Castle Place, 166 High Street, Lewes, East Sussex, England BN7 1XU
Distributed in Australia by Capricorn Link (Australia) Pty. Ltd.
P.O. Box 704, Windsor, NSW 2756, Australia

All rights reserved. No part of this publication may be reproduced,
stored in a retrieval system, or transmitted, in any form or by any means,
electronic, mechanical, photocopying, recording, or otherwise,
without prior written permission from the publisher.

Sterling ISBN 978-1-4114-3440-0

Manufactured in China

Lot #:
4 6 8 10 9 7 5 3
08/11

For information about custom editions, special sales, premium and
corporate purchases, please contact Sterling Special Sales
Department at 800-805-5489 or specialsales@sterlingpublishing.com.

Cover design and production by Mada Design, Inc.

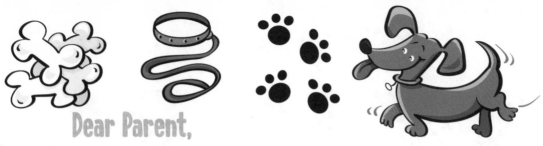

Dear Parent,

Once young children have learned to read, the next important step is to ensure that they understand and retain the information they encounter. The passages and activities contained in this book will provide your child with plenty of opportunities to develop these vital reading comprehension skills. The more your child reads and responds to literature, the greater the improvement you will see in his or her mastery of reading comprehension. To get the most from *Reading Comprehension*, follow these simple steps:

- Provide a comfortable and quiet place for your child to work.
- Encourage your child to work at his or her own pace.
- Help your child with the problems if he or she needs it.
- Offer lots of praise and support.
- Encourage your child to work independently to gain confidence in his or her problem solving skills.
- Allow your child to enjoy the fun actvities in this book.
- Most of all, remember that learning should be fun!

Visit us at *www.flashkidsbooks.com* for free downloads, informative articles, and valuable parent resources!

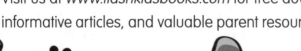

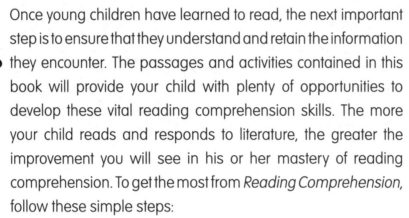

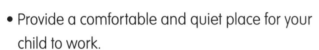

A True Talent

Brian's class was putting on a talent show. Steve asked Brian to be in a skit, and Scott invited him to sing with his band. Haley wanted Brian to help recite a poem. Brian was too nervous to be in the talent show.

"Only our families will be in the audience," Haley pointed out. "Why should you be nervous?"

Brian thought about his own family sitting in the audience. Brian's sister Kim was deaf, so she wouldn't be able to hear the show. Kim communicated with sign language, which is a way of talking with your hands. Brian had been learning sign language too. Suddenly, Brian had an idea.

Brian asked all his classmates to give him the words for their songs, skits, or poems in advance. Kim's sign language teacher helped Brian learn how to sign the words for each performance. Brian had to practice diligently to learn all the hand signs.

On the night of the show, Brian sat at the side of the stage. As each group performed, Brian signed the words. Everyone enjoyed watching Brian's sign language. Brian was talented at signing, but his true talent was being a thoughtful brother.

Answer the questions.

1. What were some of the talents Brian's classmates were planning to share?

_____

_____

2. Why didn't Brian want to perform with his classmates?

_____

_____

3. What is sign language?

_____

_____

4. How did Brian learn to sign all the words for the talent show performances?

_____

_____

5. What happened on the night of the class talent show?

_____

_____

6. Write some words that describe what type of person Brian is.

_____

_____

The Venus Flytrap

A fly looking for its next meal notices a sweet-smelling plant with big leaves shaped like clamshells. It's the perfect place for the fly to stop and drink some sweet nectar. Or is it? The fly lands on one of the leaves, and suddenly it's trapped! The leaves snap shut in less than half a second. Instead of getting a meal, the fly has become a meal for the Venus flytrap.

The Venus flytrap is a carnivorous plant, which means it eats living things. A carnivorous plant must attract, capture, kill, and digest its own food. Even so, the Venus flytrap plant has no brain, and no muscles for moving, chewing, or swallowing. So how can it move rapidly enough to gobble up insects and bugs?

The leaves of a Venus flytrap have tiny hairs that act like motion detectors. When an insect touches the hairs, it triggers the leaves to quickly snap shut, trapping and killing the insect. The leaves act as both a mouth and a stomach. They squeeze the insect tightly, and slowly the plant digests all the nutrients. About a week later, the leaves reopen and the skeleton of the insect falls out. The Venus flytrap gets ready for its next meal!

Number the steps in the correct order.

Then answer the question at the bottom.

☐ The insect touches tiny hairs that act as motion detectors.

☐ The leaves reopen and the insect's skeleton falls out.

☐ An insect lands on the leaves to drink the sweet nectar.

☐ The leaves squeeze together tightly and bring nutrients to the plant.

☐ The insect is trapped inside and dies.

☐ The hairs trigger the leaves to snap shut in less than half a second.

What is a carnivorous plant? _____

_____

Ice Climbing

Imagine that you're surrounded by ripples of frozen blue ice. Snow crunches under your boots and you dig an ice ax into what looks like a mountain of ice. This is what ice climbers do, but what they're climbing isn't really a mountain. It's a glacier, which is actually like a large, frozen river.

How are glaciers made? At very high elevations, snow builds up for years and years without ever melting. It becomes so dense that the ice looks blue. The weight of all that snow presses it together and forms a glacier. Just as river water flows downhill, the frozen snow flows downhill too. It flows very slowly over many years. As new snow falls at the top of the glacier, the entire mass slowly moves forward. Glaciers merge together and become even bigger.

In the United States, most glaciers are located in Alaska. In Juneau, Alaska, the 12-mile-long Mendenhall Glacier is easy to visit. You can get a taste for ice climbing by going on a "glacier trek." A helicopter takes tourists to a part of the glacier that is safe for climbing. Then, experienced ice climbers take them on a trek to see crystals as big as baseballs, waterfalls, ridges, and deep tunnels, all of which are made of ice. Climbing a glacier is an unforgettable adventure!

Read each statement. Write true or false.

1. A glacier is a mass of ice that's like a large frozen river. _____

2. Glaciers are formed when snow builds up and gets very dense. _____

3. Glacier snow flows downhill very quickly, just like a river. _____

4. As glaciers slowly move forward, sometimes they merge. _____

5. When glacier ice is very soft, it turns blue. _____

6. The Mendenhall Glacier is 12 miles long, so it is difficult for tourists to see. _____

7. Only experienced ice climbers can go on a glacier trek. _____

8. A helicopter takes people to a spot on the glacier that is safe to climb. _____

Polar Opposites

Not very many people have visited both the North Pole and the South Pole. Sitting at opposite ends of the earth, the two poles are 11,000 miles apart. But one special bird visits both poles every year. This bird is called the Arctic tern.

At the North Pole, called the arctic region, the Arctic tern sees a sheet of ice 6–10 feet thick and as big as the United States. What's underneath all that ice? Water! The arctic region is primarily a 3,000-foot-deep ocean covered by a layer of frozen ice. The temperature averages 0 degrees, but many animals and plants can still live here. There are 450 types of plants. Land animals, such as polar bears, foxes, and wolves, also live at the North Pole. Whales, porpoises, and seals swim in the icy water.

When the arctic tern gets to the South Pole, called the Antarctic region, it sees even more ice. The ice layer is over 7,000 feet thick, and 98% of the ice sits on top of land. Since the elevation is higher, the average temperature is –58 degrees. No land animals live here, but whales, porpoises, and seals can survive in the water. Lots of penguins live at the South Pole, but only two kinds of flowering plants grow there.

The North and South Poles are both icy and cold, but there are many differences between the two regions. Since the arctic tern visits both poles every year, it gets to see both penguins and polar bears!

Read each statement and check off whether it describes the North Pole or South Pole. If it describes both, put a check in both columns.

	North Pole (Arctic Region)	South Pole (Antarctic Region)
1. A layer of ice over 7,000 feet thick sits on top of a land mass.		
2. Whales, porpoises, and seals can swim in the water.		
3. The Arctic tern visits here every year.		
4. There are 3,000 feet of water below the ice layer.		
5. Penguins live in this region.		
6. Polar bears, wolves, and foxes live here.		
7. This pole is colder and has a higher elevation than the other pole.		
8. Lots of plants can grow here.		

The Presidents' Pets

When each United States President moves into the White House, his family goes with him. And for nearly all the presidents, his family includes his pets! Almost 400 pets, ranging from dogs and cats to bears and alligators, have called the White House home.

When the White House was first built, presidents brought their dogs and horses with them. During this time it was common for people to have barnyard animals. John Adams built the first horse stables at the White House and also had hound dogs.

People often gave animals to the president as gifts. The famous explorer Zebulon Pike gave Thomas Jefferson two bear cubs that he kept at the White House. John Quincy Adams was given an alligator, and he kept it in one of the White House bathrooms! The King of Siam gave James Buchanan a herd of elephants, which lived at the White House with two bald eagles the President already owned.

Calvin Coolidge had more pets than any other president. He kept twelve dogs at the White House, including a terrier named Peter Pan and a bulldog named Boston Beans. He also had canaries, a goose, cats, raccoons, a donkey, and a bobcat named Smokey. President Theodore Roosevelt also kept a variety of pets at the White House. He had cats, raccoons, rabbits, guinea pigs, a badger, bears, a rat, snakes, and a pig named Maude.

The White House is a special place because our nation's leaders have walked its halls, and so have their pets!

Check the facts! Read each sentence and put a check in the box if it's a fact. If the sentence is an opinion, leave the box blank.

1. Almost 400 pets have lived at the White House. ☐

2. The most interesting presidential pet was John Quincy Adam's alligator. ☐

3. Presidents often receive pets as gifts from other people. ☐

4. President Calvin Coolidge had the most creative pet names, such as "Peter Pan" and "Boston Beans." ☐

5. Theodore Roosevelt had a wide variety of pets. ☐

6. John Adams took better care of his horses than he did his hound dogs. ☐

7. John Quincy Adams should not have kept elephants at the White House. ☐

8. Thomas Jefferson had two bear cubs live at the White House. ☐

Saved by the Bell

Colleen sleepily pulled her blankets up to her chin. As the school bell rang in the distance, she jerked awake and opened her eyes. Was she dreaming, or did she really hear the bell? Colleen's school was just a block away from her house, and she would be able to hear the bell ring from her bedroom.

She glanced at her clock, but the screen was blank. Suddenly Colleen remembered unplugging her clock the night before so she could listen to CDs. She had never plugged the clock back in, so her alarm didn't go off. She had overslept. That must have been the school bell, and she was late for school!

The school bell always rang twice in the morning. At the first bell, kids were supposed to stop playing and walk to their classrooms. By the second bell, everyone should be in their seats. Colleen had a few minutes until the next bell. Could she make it?

She jumped out of bed and threw on her socks and shoes. Then she grabbed her backpack and rushed down the stairs. As Colleen ran out her front door, the last few kids were heading to their classrooms. Her heart raced as she sprinted toward the school. Just as the second bell rang, Colleen darted through the door of her classroom and slid into her seat.

"I'm lucky I heard the school bell ring," she panted. "I made it!"

"You made it in time," her friend said, "but you're still wearing your pajamas!"

Draw a line to connect each cause on the left

with its effect on the right.

1. Colleen heard the school bell ring in the distance.	a) Kids stopped playing and went to their classrooms.
2. Colleen had left her clock unplugged.	b) Her alarm didn't go off and she overslept.
3. The kids at school heard the first bell ring	c) She didn't realize she was still wearing her pajamas!
4. Colleen rushed out the door without paying attention.	d) She woke up and looked at her clock.

Batboys and Batgirls

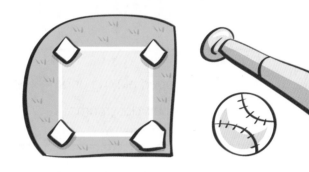

Crack! A batter hits the ball and it soars through the air. The batter tosses his bat aside and runs to first base as fast as he can. What happens to the bat that he or she left behind? It gets picked up by a batboy or batgirl. The batboy must retrieve the bat very quickly so it doesn't get in the way of the other players running the bases. It's an important job, and it doesn't stop there!

Batboys and batgirls must have a lot of energy to do their jobs well. During practice, they run after fly balls and bring them back to the players. They also fill big water jugs with ice and carry them to the field. They bring water to the umpires to quench their thirst.

You need to know a lot about baseball to be a batboy or batgirl. As soon as the first pitch is thrown, the batboy keeps track of how many baseballs the umpire has. When the umpire's supply gets low, the batboy replenishes it. Umpires often ask the batboy to bring equipment to their office. The more a batboy knows about baseball, the more helpful he can be to the team.

How do you get a job as a batboy or batgirl? Sometimes major or minor league teams put an advertisement in the newspaper. Some kids have written letters to their favorite teams, asking for a batboy job. There are also contests where you can win a prize to be a batboy or girl for one game. It's a tough job, but being part of the game and hearing the crowd roar is a big thrill!

Answer the questions.

1. After a batter hits the ball, what happens to his or her bat?

_____

2. Why do batboys and batgirls need to work quickly?

_____

3. What are some other responsibilities of batboys and batgirls?

_____

4. How do batboys and batgirls help out the umpire?

_____

5. Why do you need to know a lot about baseball?

_____

6. How can you become a batboy or batgirl?

_____

Snowman Cookies

When it's cold outside, you can warm up by baking this tasty winter treat. Making snowman cookies is just as much as fun as making a real snowman. Plus, you don't have to put on your coat and mittens to do it!

Here are the ingredients you'll need:

8 oz package of cream cheese

1 cup powdered sugar

$\frac{3}{4}$ cup butter or margarine

$\frac{1}{2}$ teaspoon vanilla

$2\frac{1}{4}$ cups flour

$\frac{1}{2}$ teaspoon baking soda

1 package mini peanut butter cups

1 can vanilla icing

Use an electric mixer to blend the cream cheese, sugar, butter, and vanilla. Then add the flour and baking soda and mix well.

Shape the dough into $\frac{1}{2}$-inch-wide small balls and 1-inch-wide large balls. Place the dough balls so they are slightly overlapping on an ungreased cookie sheet. Dip the bottom of a glass in flour, and flatten each ball of dough to $\frac{1}{4}$-inch-thick.

Bake the cookies at 325 degrees Fahrenheit for 19–21 minutes. Remove them when they are golden brown, and cool on a wire rack. Now it's time to put the snow on these snowmen. Sprinkle each cookie with powdered sugar and decorate with icing. To make snowmen hats, cut each peanut butter cup in half and place on top. Enjoy!

Number the steps in the correct order.
Then answer the question at the bottom.

☐ Shape dough into balls and place on ungreased cookie sheet.

☐ Add flour and baking soda.

☐ Bake at 325 degrees Fahrenheit for 19–21 minutes.

☐ Mix cream cheese, sugar, butter, and vanilla with electric mixer.

☐ Cut peanut butter cups in half to make hats for the snowmen.

☐ After the cookies have cooled, decorate with powdered sugar and icing.

How and when do you flatten the dough balls?

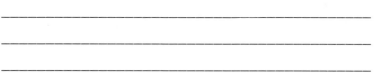

_____

_____

_____

A Dog's Best Friend

All the dogs on Ridley Street knew Connor Phillips. He was the neighborhood dog-sitter. Whenever someone was going out of town, they called Connor to take care of their dog.

Dog sitting is hard work, and Connor had to keep track of a lot of details. Each dog's owner left a list of instructions on how to take care of their dog. He had to refill the dog's food and water bowls every day. Dogs need lots of exercise, so Connor took them for walks. This was his favorite part of dog sitting. He loved putting on the dog's leash and strolling through the park. Sometimes Connor brought along a ball for the dog to play with. People stopped to pet the dog and say hello.

Connor had taken care of five different dogs on Ridley Street. He had dog-sat a German shepherd, a dachshund, a poodle, a beagle, and even a bulldog. Each dog had its own personality. Some dogs barked loudly, and others had a soft squeak. Connor's favorite dog was a dachshund named Rufus. Rufus always greeted Connor by licking his hand and wagging his tail. He liked to sit in Connor's lap and take a nap.

Although each dog was different, there was one thing they had in common. They needed lots of love and attention. Connor was good at giving that to every dog he dog-sat!

Read each statement. Write true or false.

1. Whenever Connor was going out of town,
   he called a dog-sitter.   _____

2. Connor Phillips had dog-sat five different
   dogs on Ridley Street.   _____

3. Connor's favorite part of dog sitting was refilling
   the food and water bowls.   _____

4. Dogs need to be taken on walks to get exercise.   _____

5. Connor's favorite dog was a poodle named Rufus.   _____

6. Rufus licked Connor's hand and took naps in his lap.   _____

7. Dog-sitting is very easy.   _____

8. Connor was good at giving dogs lots of love and attention.   _____

 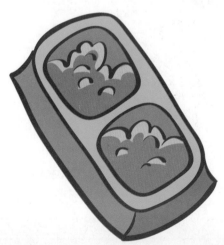

Vote for Me!

Bette and Steve are both running for class president. Read their speeches and answer the questions on the next page.

I want to be your next class president. I have been at this school for four years, and I have a lot of experience. When I was on the student council, I helped plan Career Day. I have proven that I'm organized and good with details.

If I am elected, my main goal will be to get a classroom computer. I'll plan fundraisers to buy this computer. We can also raise money to add more books to the class library. Everyone likes field trips, and I'll plan lots of field trips this year. Field trips should be fun and also help us learn.

Most importantly, I want to hear about your ideas. I'll have an idea box on the wall and anyone in the class can turn in an idea. A vote for me is a vote for a great year!

I'm new at this school, so I can bring lots of new ideas if I'm elected president. Last year, I was in charge of our class party on the last day of school. I planned a great pool party, and I can do the same for this class.

We need a class computer, and this would be my first project as your president. At my old school, we got computers donated to the class. I was on the student council and I learned all about it. I'll get a computer donated to our classroom! I also think that we should have a class pet. It's a great way to learn about animals.

The more ideas we have, the better our class will be. I would have a suggestion box for students. Please choose me as your next class president!

Read each statement and check off whether it describes Bette or Steve. If it describes both, put a check in both columns.

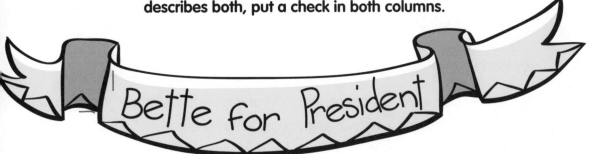

Bette for President

1. I served on the student council.

2. Having a class pet is important to me.

3. I want to get ideas from the class.

4. Getting a computer for the classroom is my goal.

5. I helped plan Career Day.

6. I want to be voted the next class president.

7. Last year, I planned a class pool party.

8. I have been at this school for four years.

Bette	Steve

Vote for Steve

Game Zone

Dear Manager,

I went to your Game Zone store on March 14 and bought the game "Wizard Battles." There's nothing better than playing video games after I've finished my homework! "Wizard Battles" is the best new game this year, and I was excited to play.

The first time I put the game in, the controls froze. I restarted the game, and I made sure the controls were all plugged in. Every time I tried to play the game, it just froze. It was really frustrating.

I brought the game back to your store on March 18. I told the salesperson that the game didn't work. He said I couldn't return the game because I had already opened the package. Then he said that my computer must be broken, or I wasn't following the directions. My computer and the game controls are not the problem. My other video games work fine. "Wizard Battles" is the only game that won't work.

This is really unfair! I have bought lots of games at Game Zone and I am a good customer. The salesperson did not treat me very nicely. The game must have been damaged when you sold it to me. Game Zone should refund my money or give me a new copy of the game.

Sincerely,

Anthony Keller

Check the facts! Read each sentence and put a check in the box if it's a fact. If the sentence is an opinion, leave the box blank.

1. Anthony bought the game "Wizard Battles" at Game Zone on March 14. ☐

2. "Wizard Battles" is the best new game of the year. ☐

3. When Anthony tried to play "Wizard Battles," the controls froze up. ☐

4. The salesperson would not let Anthony return the game. ☐

5. It was unfair for Game Zone not to let Anthony return the game. ☐

6. "Wizard Battles" was the only game that did not work on Anthony's computer. ☐

7. Anthony is Game Zone's best customer because he always shops there. ☐

8. Game Zone should give Anthony a refund or a new copy of the game. ☐

Leonardo da Vinci

Visited by nearly 6 million people every year, the "Mona Lisa" may be the most popular painting in the world. Its creator, Leonardo da Vinci, was a brilliant artist and thinker who had a big influence on art.

When Leonardo was about 14 years old, his father knew he was talented. He arranged for Leonardo to be an apprentice, or an assistant, to a well-known painter in Florence, Italy. The painter taught him how to grind and mix paint, make brushes, sculpt, and work with silver and gold. Leonardo always watched carefully and learned everything he could. By the time he was 21, Leonardo was a very skilled painter.

During this time, artists wanted paintings to look more realistic. Most paintings looked flat, and there was no sense of depth or distance. Leonardo spent a lot of time observing how people and animals really looked. He compared how objects looked up close and far away. He made lots of notes and sketches and wrote everything down in his notebook. By doing this, Leonardo figured out how to paint pictures that looked more realistic.

After he died, people wanted to study these notebooks. They had a difficult time

reading the writing. This is because Leonardo used an unusual type of writing called "mirror writing." He wrote in reverse, starting at the right side of the page and moving left. It's hard to read this writing unless you hold it up to a mirror.

Da Vinci was a fascinating man and talented artist. He helped change the way painters created artwork!

Draw a line to connect each cause on the left with its effect on the right.

1. Leonardo's father knew he had talent as an artist.	a) People have a difficult time reading his notebooks.
2. Leonardo used "mirror writing" when writing in his notebooks.	b) Leonardo's father arranged for him to be a painter's apprentice when he was about 14.
3. Painters wanted their pictures to look less flat and more realistic.	c) By the time he was 21, Leonardo was a very talented painter.
4. He learned how to mix paint, make brushes, sculpt, and work with metal.	d) Leonardo studied real people and animals and figured out how to give them depth.

Making Predictions

1. Look at the picture on the book's cover. What would be the best title for this book?

   a) Hawaiian Beaches
   b) Volcanoes of Hawaii
   c) The Hawaiian Language
   d) Planning a Hawaiian Luau

2. Circle the words that would probably appear in a paragraph about volcanoes. Cross out words that are not related.

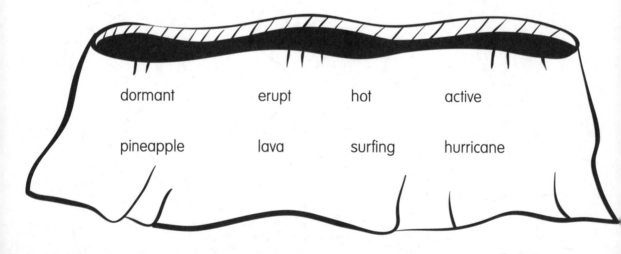

dormant	erupt	hot	active
pineapple	lava	surfing	hurricane

3. Read the Table of Contents. Which of the following might be a title for Chapter 3?

    a) Volcanoes and Hawaiian Culture

    b) Hawaiian Hula Dancing

    c) Volcanoes in the Movies

4. Read the following topic sentence:

Kilauea is not only the most active volcano in Hawaii—it's the most active volcano in the world!

According to the Table of Contents above, in which chapter would this sentence belong?

_____

TABLE OF CONTENTS

Chapter 1: How Volcanoes Created Hawaii

Chapter 2: Major Volcanic Eruptions in Hawaii

Chapter 3: _____

Chapter 4: Active Volcanoes in Hawaii Today

5. Write some things that you already know about volcanoes.

_____

_____

6. Write some things that you already know about Hawaii.

_____

_____

7. Based on the book cover and Table of Contents, would you like to read this book? Why or why not?

_____

_____

_____

One of the World's Most Active Volcanos

Kilauea is not only the most active volcano in Hawaii—it's one of the most active volcanos in the world! Lava from Kilauea has covered nearly 500 square miles during the past 1,100 years. The current eruption started in 1983 and has been going on ever since. It's the largest and longest eruption in history.

Kilauea is part of Hawaii Volcanoes National Park on the big island of Hawaii. The park helps preserve and protect these amazing volcanoes so people can study them. Tourists can visit the park and watch lava flow from Kilauea. But the volcano itself is only part of the beauty in the park. The lava flow from the park's volcanoes creates lots of natural wonders.

Black sand beaches and tree molds are two effects of lava flow. When hot lava flows into the ocean, it suddenly cools and hardens. Then it breaks into tiny black rocks, and a black sand beach is born. As lava flows downhill, it can also wrap around trees. The tree is trapped inside and the hot lava burns it out. What remains is a "tree mold"—a giant tree statue made of lava!

Kilauea is just one of many volcanoes throughout the Hawaiian Islands. In fact, the islands themselves are giant volcanoes, formed by lava that burst through the ocean floor. The eruptions that formed the islands happened millions of years ago. But if you visit Hawaii and watch lava slowly flow from Kilauea, you can get a glimpse of the same force that created the islands!

Answer the questions.

1. Why is Kilauea such an important volcano?

   _____

   _____

2. Where is Kilauea located?

   _____

   _____

3. How are black sand beaches and tree molds
   formed?

   _____

   _____

   _____

4. Explain how the Hawaiian Islands were created.

   _____

   _____

5. Would you like to visit Kilauea? Why or why not?

   _____

   _____

6. If you were going to lengthen this passage, what other things could you write
   about?

   _____

   _____

The Bake Sale

Max's soccer team was earning money to buy new uniforms. They were having a bake sale before their next soccer game to raise the money. Everyone on the team was supposed to bring something to sell. Max was planning to bake blueberry muffins with his dad.

The morning of the sale Max and his dad got up early and made the batter. While the muffins were baking in the oven, Max played with a soccer ball in the backyard. The oven timer buzzed, and Max's dad went to get the muffins. When he came back with the muffins, he looked disappointed.

"The muffins should be golden brown," said Max. "The batter hasn't cooked at all!"

"The oven didn't get hot. It must be broken," Max's dad said.

"What am I going to do?" Max said. "The bake sale is in a few hours!" Max angrily kicked his soccer ball. It rolled across the yard and bumped into a lemon tree. Max looked up and had an idea.

A few hours later, Max and his dad were carrying a huge cooler of homemade lemonade across the soccer field. They passed tables filled with cookies, brownies, cake, and homemade bread. The bake sale had already started, and everyone was munching on their treats.

"Thank goodness!" Max's soccer coach said. "Everyone is so thirsty from all these cookies. Nobody else brought anything to drink."

People rushed to buy a glass of cold lemonade. Max and his dad ran out of cups and sold every drop of their tasty beverage. Thanks to Max, everyone quenched their thirst, and the team earned enough money to buy their uniforms.

Answer the questions.

1. Why was Max's team having a bake sale?

   _____

   _____

2. What was Max planning to bring to the
   bake sale?

   _____

   _____

3. What happened on the morning of the
   bake sale?

   _____

   _____

   _____

4. How did Max get the idea to make lemonade?

   _____

   _____

5. Why was Max's coach excited about the lemonade?

   _____

   _____

6. What happened at the bake sale?

   _____

   _____

   _____

A Frozen Lollipop

Did you know that the popsicle was invented by an 11-year-old boy? His name was Frank Epperson, and he made the first popsicle by accident. The year was 1905, and the weather where Frank lived in San Francisco was colder than usual. It was popular at this time to make a drink by mixing together soda powder and water. Frank had used a stick to stir his drink. He left the drink, with the stick still in it, on his back porch overnight.

That night the temperature dropped below freezing, and Frank's soda drink froze. When he woke up, he found his drink had turned into a frozen lollipop! Using the stick as a handle, he slid his frozen drink out of his cup and called it an "Epperson Icicle." Later he changed the name to an "Epsicle."

Frank wanted to make more of his frozen lollipops, but it was difficult. It wasn't common for temperatures to drop to the freezing point in San Francisco. Frank didn't have a freezer in his home because they hadn't been invented yet! Many years later, Frank finally found a way to make and sell his Epsicles. He poured flavored juice into glass test tubes and put them into a machine that could freeze them. He even figured out a way to stamp his name on the wooden stick. His children renamed the frozen treat the Popsicle.

Frank Epperson eventually sold his popsicle invention to a dessert company, and you can still buy them in stores. In fact, people buy and eat about 3 million popsicles a year!

Number the steps in the correct order.
Then answer the question at the bottom.

[ ] Frank left his drink outside overnight and it froze.

[ ] A company bought Frank's idea for the popsicle.

[ ] Frank Epperson used a stick to mix a drink of soda powder and water.

[ ] By freezing juice in test tubes, Frank was able to make and sell Epsicles.

[ ] Frank realized he had made a tasty treat and called it an Epperson icicle.

[ ] Frank's children renamed the dessert the "popsicle."

Why was it difficult at first for Frank to make more Epsicles and sell them?

_____

_____

_____

_____

_____

_____

_____

_____

Television Time!

6:00

4	News
5	Cartoons
7	*School Blues:* A comedy about a blues singer who becomes a school principal.
12	News

6:30

4	Talk of the Town! Guest: Professional Dancer Kara Sandberg
5	Special News Report: "Overcrowded Schools: Soaring Class Sizes in the City"
12	Music Videos

7:00

4	NFL Football: San Diego Chargers vs. Denver Broncos
5	Grow Your Garden: "All About Roses"
12	Cartoons

8:00

5	National Spelling Bee: Students from across the country compete for the championship.
7	News
12	*Playing It Right:* A romance about two piano players competing for the same prize.

Read each statement. Write true or false.

1. Channels 4 and 12 both have the news at 6:00.   _____

2. A gardening show is on channel 5 at 7:00.   _____

3. You can watch a romance movie on channel 7.   _____

4. Music videos are shown on channel 12 for an hour.   _____

6. The movie *School Blues* is 2 hours long.   _____

7. You can watch football at 7:00 on channel 4.   _____

8. Channels 12 and 5 both show cartoons at
   the same time.   _____

Happy Halloween

GHOST STORIES

GAMES & PRIZES

Haunted Hut
at The Community Clubhouse
October 30 & 31
7:00 PM to 10:00 PM

You'll have a scream at this year's Haunted Hut party! Get spooked at the scariest Haunted House in town, or bob for apples in our Halloween Game Hut. Don't miss out on the costume contest—this year's winner will receive two free movie passes!

Ages 8 and up only!
Admission: $1.00
No charge for anyone wearing a costume!

COSTUME CONTEST

HAUNTED HOUSE

PUMPKIN CARVING

Halloween Bash
at Centerville Park
Halloween Night Only!
October 31
7:00 PM – 10:00 PM

This Halloween, head to Centerville Park for the annual Halloween Bash! Our Halloween Bash has everything from a Haunted House to a sing-a-long for the whole family. Munch on yummy treats such hot dogs, hamburgers, and ice cream sundaes. Lots of activities for all ages, including:

- Pumpkin Carving
- Spooky Song Sing-A-Long
- Refreshments
- Haunted House
- Costume Parade and Contest

All Ages Welcome!
Admission is $1.00 per person, or wear your costume to get in free!

Read each statement and check off whether it describes the Halloween Bash or the Haunted Hut.

If it describes both, put a check in both boxes.

	Halloween Bash	Haunted Hut

1. Admission is free for anyone wearing a costume.

2. The winner of the costume contest wins two movie passes.

3. A spooky sing-a-long will be held.

4. You can listen to ghost stories.

5. Refreshments such as hot dogs and hamburgers will be available.

6. This event is only for kids ages 8 and up.

7. A costume contest will be held.

8. You can do pumpkin carving at this event.

How Do You Get to School?

Wayview School Newspaper

WAYS TO GET TO WAYVIEW

How did you get to school today? A recent poll of the school reveals that Wayview students get to school by riding the bus, driving, biking, walking, and riding a scooter.

Our poll shows that 25% of Wayview students take the bus to school. Fourth grade student Wesley Gibson explained, "The bus is the best way to get to school. I can relax and chat with my friends while the bus driver does all the work. Sometimes I even finish my homework on the bus!" Another 25% of Wayview students are driven to school by their parents every day. In all, 50% of Wayview students get to school in a vehicle, either the bus or a car.

The other 50% of Wayview students ride their bikes, walk, or ride a scooter. Fifth-grader Alexis Wang is one of the 20% of Wayside students who walk to school each day. She said, "Walking to school is better than the bus or car because you get more exercise." Another 20% of Wayview students ride their bikes.

Chris Madsen said he likes riding his bike because "it's faster than walking, and you can race with your friends."

The last group of Wayview students gets to school by riding scooters. The number of students riding scooters to school has increased. Last year, only 5% of the students rode scooters, and this year it's 10%. Ella Peterson said, "Riding a scooter is the most fun way to get to school. It's as fast as a bike, and scooters are cool." Principal Wang wanted to remind all Wayview students that anyone riding a bike or scooter to school must wear a helmet.

As you can see, Wayview students find all kinds of ways to get to school. In the end it doesn't really matter how you get here, as long you get here on time!

Check the facts! Read each sentence and put a check in the box if it's a fact. If the sentence is an opinion, leave the box blank.

1. Half of the students at Wayview get to school by bus or car. ☐

2. Chris Madsen is one of the students who rides his bike to school every day. ☐

3. It is better to walk to school than to take the bus or ride in a car. ☐

4. The bus is the best way to get to school because you can relax and do your homework. ☐

5. The principal wants anyone riding a bike or scooter to school to wear a helmet. ☐

6. Riding a scooter is the most fun way to get to school. ☐

7. Alexis Wang is one of the 20% of students who walk to school. ☐

8. Only 10% of the students at Wayview ride a scooter to school. ☐

Where Do Diamonds Come from?

Have you ever walked past a jewelry store and seen sparkling diamonds on display? Perhaps you've wondered why diamonds are so expensive and where they come from. A diamond's journey to the jewelry store is very long, and it starts deep within the earth.

Diamonds form about 100 miles beneath the earth's surface inside the mantle. If the temperature and pressure are just right, carbon atoms can turn into diamonds. It takes about 5 gigapascals of pressure and a temperature of 2,200 degrees Fahrenheit for a diamond to form. This process takes thousands of years.

Once a diamond is formed, it still has to get to the surface. How do diamonds travel 100 miles upward? Liquid rock called magma acts like an elevator and carries them up to the surface. Once on the earth's surface, the magma cools and hardens into rock. People find the diamonds buried deep within rocks. Sometimes water erodes, or wears away, the hardened magma, and then the diamonds wash up in rivers or streams.

Diamonds are valuable because they are so rare and special. They are also valuable because they are very strong. When the atoms of carbon form into a diamond, they bond

together very tightly. This makes diamonds one of the strongest substances on earth. In fact, the word "diamond" comes from the Greek word *adamas*, which means "indestructible." Next time you see a diamond in a jewelry store, think of how far it had to travel to get there!

Draw a line to connect each cause on the left

with its effect on the right.

1. Liquid magma carries diamonds to the earth's surface and then hardens.
2. Deep in the earth's mantle, the temperature and pressure reach a certain point.
3. Water erodes the rock around the diamond.
4. When carbon turns into diamonds, the atoms bond very tightly.

a) Diamonds wash up in rivers and streams.
b) Diamonds are indestructible and very valuable.
c) People find diamonds in rocks.
d) Carbon atoms turn into diamonds.

Super Singers

Imagine yourself singing in front of an audience, performing in other countries, and having your music put on a CD! All this excitement isn't just for rock stars. Joining a children's chorus gives kids the chance to do these exciting activities. What does it take to get into a children's chorus? You don't need years of singing lessons. You just need to have a love for singing and be willing to learn and follow directions.

It all starts at the audition. The choirmaster, or conductor, will have you sing with a group of kids. As the group sings, the conductor listens to how your voice blends in. You'll also probably be asked to sing solo, or by yourself. The conductor wants to figure out what type of voice you have. A girl with a high voice is a *soprano* while a girl with a low voice is an *alto*. A boy with a high voice is a *tenor*, while a boy with a low voice is a *bass*. When the whole chorus sings together, the different types of voices sing different notes to the same song. This is called "singing parts."

Once you pass the audition, you might be assigned to a specific group. Beginning singers are often grouped together in a "Treble Chorus." More advanced singers might be in a "Concert Chorus." Different choirs have different names for these groups. The more advanced groups learn harder songs and perform more. No matter which group you're in, you'll need to go to rehearsals. Most children's choirs rehearse once a week.

Answer the questions.

1. What skills do you need to join a children's chorus?

_____

_____

2. What happens at the audition?

_____

_____

3. What's the difference between *soprano* and *alto*?

_____

_____

4. What does it mean to "sing parts"?

_____

_____

5. What's the difference between a "Treble Chorus" and a "Concert Chorus"?

_____

_____

6. How often do most children's choirs rehearse?

_____

_____

Cleaning Up the Fast Way

When Travis and Jake opened the door to Travis's bedroom, they saw something they didn't like. Travis's mother stood in the middle of the room with her hands on her hips.

"Travis, you were supposed to clean your room before Jake got here," his mother said.

"I forgot," Travis said. "Can't I do it later?"

"No," she said. "You need to do it now. Jake can wait downstairs while you clean up."

"I'll help Travis," Jake said. "I know how to clean up the fast way."

"I hope it is fast. In thirty minutes, Jake will have to go home if the room isn't clean," Travis's mother said as she shut the door.

"We'll never finish in time," Travis said.

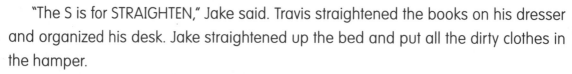

"We just have to work fast—F.A.S.T." Jake said. "Listen up. The F in 'fast' is for FLOOR. The A is for AWAY. Let's pick everything up off the *floor* and put it *away.*"

The boys picked up the shoes, books, and toys that littered the floor and put everything away. The room looked better, but there was still stuff on the bed, dresser, and desk.

"The S is for STRAIGHTEN," Jake said. Travis straightened the books on his dresser and organized his desk. Jake straightened up the bed and put all the dirty clothes in the hamper.

"I didn't realize how much garbage I had everywhere," Travis said.

"Perfect," Jake said. "The T in 'fast' is for TRASH."

The boys threw broken toys, papers, and wrappers in the trash. Just as Travis was about to take out the trash, his mother appeared in the doorway.

"Wow," she said. "The room looks great! What's your secret?"

"Jake just showed me how to work fast," Travis said, smiling at Jake.

Number the steps in the correct order.
Then answer the question at the bottom.

☐ The boys picked up everything off the floor and put it away.

☐ Travis straightened his desk and Jake straightened the bed.

☐ Travis's mother told him he had to clean his room right away.

☐ The room looked better, but the bed and dresser were still messy.

☐ Travis's mom came back and said the room looked great.

☐ The boys threw a bunch of garbage in the trash.

What do the letters in FAST stand for?

_____

_____

_____

_____

How Coyote Stole Fire

The Native Americans have many stories about a man named Coyote. Coyote tried to help others and do good deeds, but he was also a trickster. One day Coyote passed a group of crying women. They were singing a sad song for all the people who had died during the long, cold winter. Man did not yet have fire, and many people died from the cold every winter.

"The sun brings us warmth," said one of the crying women. "If we could have a small piece of sun in our teepees during the winter months, we could keep warm." Coyote felt their sadness and wanted to help. He knew of three Fire Beings who lived on a mountaintop. They selfishly kept fire all to themselves. The Fire Beings did not want to share fire with man, because they didn't want man to become more powerful.

Coyote went to the Fire Beings' mountain and observed how they guarded their fire. He noticed that during the night, the Fire Beings took turns watching their fire. When it was time to change guards, one Fire Being went into a teepee. A few moments would pass before the next one came out for his turn. During that time nobody watched the fire. Coyote waited until no one was watching, then he snatched up a piece of the glowing fire. He bolted down the mountain and the Fire Beings raced after him.

Coyote threw the fire to his animal friends, and they threw it to Wood. Then Wood swallowed the fire. The Fire Beings offered Wood gifts, but Wood didn't give up the fire.

Finally the Fire Beings gave up and went back to their mountain.

Coyote knew how to get fire out of Wood. He showed man how to rub two sticks together to create fire. Man now had a "piece of the sun" to stay warm during the winter.

Read each statement. Write true or false.

1. Coyote only wanted to fool and hurt people. _____

2. Coyote felt sorry for man because he had
   no fire to stay warm in the winter. _____

3. Three Fire Beings kept fire all to themselves up on
   a mountaintop. _____

4. Coyote watched the Fire Beings and looked for a
   chance to steal the fire. _____

5. The Fire Beings guarded the fire and never left it
   alone for a moment. _____

6. When Coyote stole a piece of fire, the Fire Beings
   chased after him. _____

7. The Fire Beings convinced Wood to give up the fire. _____

8. Coyote taught man how to rub sticks together to
   make fire. _____

How Raven Stole Light

The native people of Alaska have a story about a creature named Raven who brought light into the world. As the story goes, a long time ago there was no light in the world. Everyone lived in darkness. An old man and his daughter were secretly hiding all the light. Inside their house three bags hung on the wall. One bag held the stars, one held the moon, and one held daylight. Raven made a plan to get the bags.

Raven turned himself into the baby of the old man's daughter. The old man thought Raven was his grandson and loved him very much. When Raven cried for the bags on the wall, the old man wanted to make him happy. Finally, the old man gave Raven the bag of stars to make him stop crying.

Raven pushed the bag of stars over to the fireplace and untied the knots. The stars flew out the chimney and up into the sky. The old man and his daughter were sad to lose the stars, but they thought it was just an accident.

Raven did not stop at the stars. He kept crying until the old man could stand it no longer. This time the old man gave Raven the bag with the moon. Raven pushed it toward the fireplace and let the moon fly up into the sky. Still, the old man thought Raven was just a baby.

Raven cried so loud for the last bag that the old man gave it to him. The last bag held daylight. This time, Raven flew out the chimney with the bag. As daylight filled the sky, the old man and his daughter knew they had been tricked. They were angry that Raven had stolen their light. Everyone else was glad, for Raven had brought them out of darkness and given light to the world.

Read each statement and check off whether it describes Raven or Coyote.

If it describes both, put a check in both columns.

	Raven	Coyote
1. He is a "trickster" who both fools and helps people.		
2. He wanted to give man a gift that would make life easier.		
3. He felt sad for the people who died during the cold winter months.		
4. He stole something that was being kept from man.		
5. He turned himself into a baby as part of his trick.		
6. He stole a piece of fire from the Fire Beings.		
7. He cried until the old man gave him all the bags.		
8. He showed man how to rub sticks together and make fire.		

Book Report

Frindle
By Andrew Clements

The book *Frindle* is about a troublemaker named Nick who makes up a new word. His teacher, Mrs. Granger, really likes the dictionary. When Nick asks Mrs. Granger where all the words in the dictionary came from, she makes Nick write a report about it! The report makes Nick wonder if he could invent his own word. Nick's classmate Janet drops her pen, and he picks it up and calls it a "frindle." Pretty soon, everyone in class is saying "frindle" instead of pen.

A war begins between Mrs. Granger and Nick. Nick likes to challenge the rules, but he's not all bad. He is creative and has lots of ideas. It's too bad that people think something is wrong just because it's new and different. Mrs. Granger is too hard on Nick and the way she treats him is unfair.

The best part is when the kids in Nick's class stick up for him. They are even willing to stay after school and be punished for saying "frindle." When a class sticks together like that it's really special.

Mrs. Granger wants to stop Nick from spreading his word. But the "frindle" is unstoppable. People across the country are saying it. Nick gets a lot of attention for inventing this word. He sees that one person can have a big effect.

The book has a very surprising ending. Nick is in college, and he is rich from all the money he has made off his word. Mrs. Granger sends him a dictionary that has the word "frindle" and a letter about how she is proud of him. She ends up being the most interesting character in the book!

Everyone should read *Frindle* because it's such a great book. Kids who are troublemakers would especially like this book.

Check the facts! Read each sentence and put a check in the box if it's a fact. If the sentence is an opinion, leave the box blank.

1. The book *Frindle* is about a boy named Nick who creates a new word. ☐

2. After Nick calls a pen a "frindle," everyone starts saying his new word. ☐

3. The best part of the book is when Nick's classmates stick up for Nick and his word. ☐

4. Everyone, especially kids who are troublemakers, should read *Frindle*. ☐

5. At the end, Mrs. Granger sends Nick a letter saying she is proud. ☐

6. People should not think something is wrong just because it's new or different. ☐

7. Nick gets a lot of attention and even gets rich off the money he makes from his word. ☐

8. Mrs. Granger is the most interesting character in the book. ☐

The Chore Chart

Justin's stomach growled as he searched the cabinet. Once again, he couldn't find a clean bowl, and the dishwasher was full of dirty dishes. Justin wanted cereal for breakfast, but he'd have to find something else. As he grabbed a cup of yogurt from the fridge, his brother Alex stumbled into the kitchen.

"I almost tripped over that bag! Why didn't you take out the trash?" Alex said.

"Ethan is supposed to take out the trash," Justin said.
"I guess he forgot."

"How can I take out the trash when I can't find my clothes?" Ethan said, popping his head out of the laundry room. He was still wearing his pajamas.

"What's all this commotion?" the boys' dad asked.

"Everyone needs to pitch in around the house," Mom said. "It seems like nobody can remember what their chores are."

"Why don't we make a chore chart?" their dad suggested. "We can rotate the chores every week. The chart will make it clear who is supposed to do what."

"Nobody will have any excuse for not doing their chore," Mom added.

The family made a circular chart that looked like a wheel. Justin, Alex, Ethan, Mom, and Dad's names were all in the wheel. On the outside, they listed five chores: Do Dishes, Take out Trash, Fold Laundry, Mow Lawn, and Sweep.

The chore chart helped everyone know exactly what they were supposed to do that week. The boys didn't argue over who was supposed to do what. There were always clean bowls for cereal, nobody tripped over the trash bags, and the laundry room had piles of neatly folded clothes. The chore chart made everything a lot easier!

Draw a line to connect each cause on the left with its effect on the right.

1. Justin couldn't find any clean bowls in the kitchen.	a) He didn't take out the trash, and Alex almost tripped over the bag.
2. The boys' parents wanted everyone to remember their chores.	b) They made a chart showing everyone's names and five different chores.
3. The family made a chore chart to show who should do what.	c) He couldn't have cereal for breakfast.
4. The laundry wasn't sorted and Ethan couldn't find his clothes.	d) The boys didn't argue and all the chores got done.

Thomas Jefferson

Thomas Jefferson was the third president of the United States. Although he was president only from 1801 to 1809, he served the country his entire life. Jefferson was an important leader who helped shape America.

Jefferson went to college in Williamsburg, Virginia, which was the capital of the colonies at that time. He learned a lot about government and studied law. He was a good student, and he learned French, Spanish, and Italian. He even built his own house and called it Monticello, which means "little mountain" in Italian.

Although Jefferson didn't like to speak in public, he was a very good writer. He used his writing skill to help America gain independence from Britain. He wrote the Declaration of Independence, which began the Revolutionary War.

Before he ran for president, Jefferson was Governor of Virginia and was also a member of Congress. Even though he was very popular, becoming president was tough. The first time he ran for president he lost by three votes. He became John Adams's Vice President. In 1800, Jefferson ran again. This time Jefferson won.

During the years he was president, Thomas Jefferson doubled the size of the United States. He bought some land in the west that was owned by France. This event was called the Louisiana Purchase.

Even after his time as president was over, Jefferson continued to work hard. He founded the University of Virginia and designed the school buildings himself. Thomas Jefferson died on July 4, 1826, exactly 50 years after the Declaration of Independence was written. When we celebrate the Fourth of July, we can also honor Thomas Jefferson and everything he did for the country.

A summary should cover the major ideas from the reading passge.
Circle the best summary of the reading passage
about Thomas Jefferson.

a) Thomas Jefferson must have been a very persistent person. The fist time he ran for president he lost by only three votes! He became the Vice President to John Adams. Even when Jefferson ran again, it was a tie. It took time for congress to figure out who should be president. Jefferson had received the majority of the votes, so he was declared the next president. Because Jefferson didn't give up, he was able to become president.

b) Although Jefferson didn't like to speak in public, he had other talents. Thomas Jefferson was a very talented builder. He even built his own house, which he called Monticello. Monticello actually means "little mountain" in Italian. Jefferson had studied Italian in school, and he also learned French and Spanish. Later in his life he designed buildings for the University of Virginia. He helped our nation by being such a great builder.

c) Thomas Jefferson was a lifelong American leader. He wrote the Declaration of Independence, which helped America break free from Britain. Before becoming president, Jefferson was the governor of Virginia, a congressman, and vice president to John Adams. As the third president, Jefferson doubled the size of the country through the Louisiana Purchase. Throughout his life, Jefferson used his talents to help the country.

Mapmaking

Imagine if your job was to explore new lands, name the mountains and rivers, and then capture it all on paper. That's exactly what a cartographer, or mapmaker, does. Early cartographers made maps by hand with brushes and parchment. They also printed maps on wood blocks and hand colored them. Maps were very valuable. George Washington was a mapmaker! Today computers help cartographers work quickly, and anyone can buy a map. Still, the basic steps of mapmaking are the same as they were years ago.

The cartographer's first step is to figure out the location of the area. He notes all the features in the area, such as buildings, rivers, or mountains. This is called "surveying" the land. A cartographer uses an imaginary grid of numbered lines that divides up the earth to figure out the latitude and longitude of the location.

The next step is to make a scale for the map. The area being mapped might be huge, but the map is only a small piece of paper. The scale tells people how the distance on paper relates to the real distance on the ground. For example, a map's scale might show that 1 inch on the map equals 100 miles on the ground.

The third step is to add symbols to the map. A cartographer might use a tree to show a forest or an airplane to show where an airport is. A key or legend at the bottom of the map shows what the symbols mean. The final step is naming things. Many of our mountains, lakes, and rivers were named by early explorers. Today, a cartographer might help name the streets in a town or city.

Thanks to cartographers, we can find our way through cities and countries, mountains and deserts, or even just through the mall!

Write a summary of the reading passage about mapmaking. Remember, a summary should briefly cover all the major ideas in the passage.

_____
_____
_____
_____
_____
_____
_____
_____
_____
_____
_____
_____
_____
_____
_____
_____
_____
_____
_____
_____
_____
_____

Creative Writing

Understanding literary elements such as characters, setting, conflict, and plot will help you become a better reader. Use the worksheet below to brainstorm ideas for your own story.

Characters: Who are the people that will be in your story?
Write down their names and describe them.

_____

_____

_____

Setting: Where will your story take place?

_____

_____

_____

Conflict: What problem does your character face?

_____

_____

_____

Plot: What might happen as the character tries to overcome that problem?

_____

_____

_____

_____

_____

Use your ideas on page 60 to write your own story.
Remember to use lots of details and give your story a title.

_____

_____

_____

_____

_____

_____

_____

_____

_____

_____

_____

_____

_____

_____

_____

_____

_____

_____

_____

_____

_____

_____

_____

Answer Key

Page 5
1. Steve was doing a skit, Scott was singing, and Haley was reciting a poem.
2. He was nervous about singing or speaking in front of an audience.
3. Sign language is a way of using hand signs to talk.
4. He asked for all the words in advance, and Kim's teacher taught him the signs.
5. Brian signed the words to all the performances, and everyone enjoyed watching.
6. Answers will vary. Answers may include: thoughtful, hard-working, caring.

Page 7
2 The insect touches tiny hairs that act as motion detectors.
6 The leaves reopen and the insect's skeleton falls out.
1 An insect lands on the leaves to drink the sweet nectar.
5 The leaves squeeze together tightly and bring nutrients to the plant.
4 The insect is trapped inside and dies.
3 The hairs trigger the leaves to snap shut in less than half a second.

A carnivorous plant eats living things by attracting, capturing, killing, and digesting them.

Page 9
1. true
2. true
3. false
4. true
5. false
6. false
7. false
8. true

Page 11
1. South Pole
2. both
3. both
4. North Pole
5. South Pole
6. North Pole
7. South Pole
8. North Pole

Page 13
1. fact
2. opinion
3. fact
4. opinion
5. fact
6. opinion
7. opinion
8. fact

Page 15
1. d
2. b
3. a
4. c

Page 17
1. He throws the bat to the side and runs the bases.
2. So the bat doesn't get in the way of other players on the field.
3. They run after fly balls, carry jugs of ice to the field, and bring water to the umpire.
4. The batboy replenishes the umpire's supply of balls and helps carry equipment.
5. The more you know about baseball, the more helpful you can be.
6. You can respond to a newspaper ad, write the team a letter, or win a contest.

Page 19
3 Shape dough into balls and place on ungreased cookie sheet.
2 Add flour and baking soda.
4 Bake at 325 degrees Fahrenheit for 19–21 minutes.
1 Mix cream cheese, sugar, butter, and vanilla with electric mixer.
6 Cut peanut butter cups in half to make hats for the snowmen.
5 After the cookies have cooled, decorate with powdered sugar and icing.

After the dough balls are on the cookie sheet, dip the bottom of a glass in flour and push on the dough to flatten it.

Page 21
1. false
2. true
3. false
4. true
5. false
6. true
7. false
8. true

Page 23
1. both
2. Steve
3. both
4. both
5. Bette
6. both
7. Steve
8. Bette

Page 25
1. fact
2. opinion
3. fact
4. fact
5. opinion
6. fact
7. opinion
8. opinion

Page 27
1. b
2. a
3. d
4. c

Page 28
1. b
2. These words are circled: dormant, erupt, active, lava, hot

Page 29
3. a
4. Chapter 4
5. Answers will vary.
6. Answers will vary.
7. Answers will vary.

Page 31
1. Kilauea is one of the most active volcanos in the world.
2. It's located on the big island of Hawaii inside Hawaii Volcanoes National Park.
3. When lava hits the ocean, it forms a black sand beach. When lava wraps around a tree, the tree inside burns and the lava makes a tree mold.
4. Lava burst through the ocean floor and created a chain of islands.
5. Answers will vary.
6. Answers will vary.

Page 33
1. The bake sale was to raise money for new uniforms.

Answer Key

2. He was planning to bring blueberry muffins.
3. The oven broke so the muffins did not cook.
4. He kicked his soccer ball and it rolled into the lemon tree.
5. Nobody had brought anything to drink and everyone was thirsty.
6. Max and his dad sold every drop of their lemonade and ran out of cups.

Page 35
2 Frank left his drink outside overnight and it froze.
6 A company bought Frank's idea for the popsicle.
1 Frank Epperson used a stick to mix a drink of soda powder and water.
4 By freezing juice in test tubes, Frank was able to make and sell Epsicles.
3 Frank realized he had made a tasty treat and called it an Epperson icicle.
5 Frank's children renamed the dessert the "popsicle."

There was no way to freeze the popsicles. The temperature in San Francisco rarely dropped low enough, and freezers had not yet been invented.

Page 37
1. true
2. true
3. false
4. false
6. true
7. true
8. false

Page 39
1. both

2. Haunted Hut
3. Halloween Bash
4. Haunted Hut
5. Halloween Bash
6. Haunted Hut
7. both
8. both

Page 41
1. fact
2. fact
3. opinion
4. opinion
5. fact
6. opinion
7. fact
8. fact

Page 43
1. c
2. d
3. a
4. b

Page 45
1. To be in a choir you need to love singing and be able to follow directions.
2. At the audition, you sing with a group and by yourself.
3. A soprano sings high notes and an alto sings low notes.
4. Singing parts is when the sopranos and altos sing different notes to the same song.
5. A "Treble Chorus" is for beginning singers and "Concert Chorus" is for more advanced singers. A "Concert Chorus" usually performs more.
6. Most children's choirs rehearse once a week.

Page 47
2 The boys picked up

everything off the floor and put it away.
4 Travis straightened his desk and Jake straightened the bed.
1 Travis's mother told him he had to clean his room right away.
3 The room looked better, but the bed and dresser were still messy.
6 Travis's mom came back and said the room looked great.
5 The boys threw a bunch of garbage in the trash.

FAST stands for Floor, Away, Straighten, and Trash.

Page 49
1. false
2. true
3. true
4. true
5. false
6. true
7. false
8. true

Page 51
1. both
2. both
3. Coyote
4. both
5. Raven
6. Coyote
7. Raven
8. Coyote

Page 53
1. fact
2. fact
3. opinion
4. opinion
5. fact
6. opinion
7. fact
8. opinion

Page 55
1. c
2. b
3. d
4. a

Page 57
The best summary is c.

Page 59
Answers will vary.

Page 60
Answers will vary.

Page 61
Answers will vary.

CHAMPION

Nice work!

_____ ,
(Name)

you're a
reading
champion!